Sober As F***

THE DAILY SOBRIETY TRACKER & JOURNAL

Sober As F***

THE DAILY SOBRIETY TRACKER AND JOURNAL

ISBN: 9781098841461

Hey Y'all,

I'm pretty f***ing excited about this one!

Y'all have built the whole *Sober As F*** book series into what it is today. It's been so beautiful to watch other people in the world going through sobriety together and connecting over the book and the workbook. I wanted to give you guys something else to add to the arsenal of tools you can use to crush the f*** out of your sobriety. That's how this little baby came to life!

I have seen SO many people using Apps on their phone to track their sobriety. They are super popular and convenient, BUT there are some of us out there that like something that is real, concrete, and we can touch and hold. I also believe in the therapeutic power and accountability of writing things down...because, duh, I'm a writer!

I created this tracker and journal to be a tool you can use daily to count your days, track your emotional journey, gain a little inspo when things get tough, and let it all out with some journaling.

Sobriety isn't always easy, but if we work our a** off at it every single day, we can absolutely be succussful in it. Using the help and tools that are available for you can make it a little bit easier. So use the f*** out of this!

my sober date:

February 23, 2022

my WHY:

WHY DO YOU WANT TO BE SOBER?
THINK OF THIS AS YOUR "MISSION STATEMENT" &
MOTIVATION YOU CAN COME BACK TO WHEN THINGS
GET HARD.

I want to be sober so I can be the best version of myself. I want to stay connected to my HP, myself, and of course my boys. I want to be sober so I can be so spritualy fit I can handle anything. I want to be able to provide a beautiful life for my boys and me. I want to be sober because I love myself and I deserve to live a clean & happy life.

There is not a person on the planet that is not recovering from something, and that the process of recovery is about regaining oneself from whatever it is that may have stolen us.

-Jada Pinkett Smith

date: _____

NOTHING CHANGES IF NOTHING CHANGES.

Days Sober:

I FEEL : _____

■ ■

MY GOALS FOR TODAY ARE:

_____
_____
_____
_____
_____

TODAY I'M GRATEFUL FOR:

1.

2.

3.

4.

I Will Support My Sobriety Today By:

DO I FEEL ANY URGES/CRAVINGS TODAY?

YES   NO

☐   ☐

today i...

_____

_____

_____

_____

_____

_____

_____

_____

_____

_____

_____

_____

_____

_____

_____

_____

_____

_____

date: _____

DAILY MANTRA:

ONE DAY AT A TIME.

Days Sober:

I FEEL : _____

■ ■

MY GOALS FOR TODAY ARE:

_____
_____
_____
_____
_____

TODAY I'M GRATEFUL FOR:

1.

2.

3.

4.

I Will Support My Sobriety Today By:

DO I FEEL ANY URGES/CRAVINGS TODAY?

YES   NO

☐   ☐

today i...

_____
_____
_____
_____
_____
_____
_____
_____
_____
_____
_____
_____
_____
_____
_____
_____
_____
_____
_____
_____

date: _____

I'M STRIVING FOR PROGRESS, NOT PERFECTION.

Days Sober:

I FEEL : _____

■ ■ ■ ■ ■ ■ ■ ■ ■ ■ ■ ■ ■ ■ ■ ■ ■ ■ ■ ■

MY GOALS FOR TODAY ARE:

_____

_____

_____

_____

_____

TODAY I'M GRATEFUL FOR:

1.

2.

3.

4.

I Will Support My Sobriety Today By:

DO I FEEL ANY URGES/CRAVINGS TODAY?

YES   NO

☐   ☐

today i...

_____
_____
_____
_____
_____
_____
_____
_____
_____
_____
_____
_____
_____
_____
_____
_____
_____
_____
_____

date: _____

DAILY MANTRA:

IF I WANT WHAT I'VE
NEVER HAD, I MUST DO
WHAT I'VE NEVER
DONE.

Days Sober:

I FEEL : _____

■ ■

MY GOALS FOR TODAY ARE:

_____
_____
_____
_____
_____

TODAY I'M GRATEFUL FOR:

1.

2.

3.

4.

**I Will Support My
Sobriety Today By:**

DO I FEEL ANY
URGES/CRAVINGS
TODAY?

YES   NO

☐   ☐

today i...

_____

_____

_____

_____

_____

_____

_____

_____

_____

_____

_____

_____

_____

_____

_____

_____

_____

_____

_____

_____

_____

date: _____

DAILY MANTRA:

I'M GROWING THROUGH WHAT I'M GOING THROUGH.

Days Sober:

I FEEL : _____

■ ■

MY GOALS FOR TODAY ARE:

_____
_____
_____
_____

TODAY I'M GRATEFUL FOR:

1.

2.

3.

4.

I Will Support My Sobriety Today By:

DO I FEEL ANY URGES/CRAVINGS TODAY?

YES

NO

today i...

_____
_____
_____
_____
_____
_____
_____
_____
_____
_____
_____
_____
_____
_____
_____
_____
_____
_____
_____
_____

date: _____

DAILY MANTRA:

I AM IN CONTROL
OF MY OWN LIFE.

Days Sober:

I FEEL : _____

■ ■

MY GOALS FOR TODAY ARE:

_____
_____
_____

_____
_____

TODAY I'M GRATEFUL FOR:

1.

2.

3.

4.

**I Will Support My
Sobriety Today By:**

DO I FEEL ANY
URGES/CRAVINGS
TODAY?

YES   NO

today i...

_____

_____

_____

_____

_____

_____

_____

_____

_____

_____

_____

_____

_____

_____

_____

_____

_____

_____

_____

date: _____

DAILY MANTRA:

EVERY DAY IN
EVERY WAY, I AM
GETTING BETTER.

Days Sober:

I FEEL : _____

MY GOALS FOR TODAY ARE:

_____
_____
_____
_____
_____

TODAY I'M GRATEFUL FOR:

1.

2.

3.

4.

I Will Support My Sobriety Today By:

DO I FEEL ANY
URGES/CRAVINGS
TODAY?

YES   NO

☐   ☐

today i...

_____

_____

_____

_____

_____

_____

_____

_____

_____

_____

_____

_____

_____

_____

_____

_____

_____

_____

Only an addict can understand how lonely beginning recovery feels...how overwhelming it all seems.

-Robert Downey Jr.

date: _____

NOTHING CHANGES IF NOTHING CHANGES.

Days Sober:

I FEEL : _____

■ ■

MY GOALS FOR TODAY ARE:

_____
_____
_____
_____
_____

TODAY I'M GRATEFUL FOR:

1.

2.

3.

4.

I Will Support My Sobriety Today By:

DO I FEEL ANY URGES/CRAVINGS TODAY?

YES   NO

☐   ☐

today i...

_____

_____

_____

_____

_____

_____

_____

_____

_____

_____

_____

_____

_____

_____

_____

_____

_____

_____

_____

_____

_____

_____

date: _____

DAILY MANTRA:

ONE DAY AT A TIME.

Days Sober:

I FEEL : _____

■ ■ ■ ■ ■ ■ ■ ■ ■ ■ ■ ■ ■ ■ ■ ■ ■ ■ ■

MY GOALS FOR TODAY ARE:

_____
_____
_____
_____
_____

TODAY I'M GRATEFUL FOR:

1.

2.

3.

4.

I Will Support My Sobriety Today By:

DO I FEEL ANY URGES/CRAVINGS TODAY?

YES

NO

today i...

_____

_____

_____

_____

_____

_____

_____

_____

_____

_____

_____

_____

_____

_____

_____

_____

_____

_____

_____

_____

_____

date: _____

DAILY MANTRA:

I'M STRIVING FOR PROGRESS, NOT PERFECTION.

Days Sober:

I FEEL : _____

■ ■

MY GOALS FOR TODAY ARE:

_____

_____

_____

_____

_____

TODAY I'M GRATEFUL FOR:

1.

2.

3.

4.

I Will Support My Sobriety Today By:

DO I FEEL ANY URGES/CRAVINGS TODAY?

YES   NO

☐   ☐

today i...

_____

_____

_____

_____

_____

_____

_____

_____

_____

_____

_____

_____

_____

_____

_____

_____

_____

_____

_____

_____

_____

date: _____

Days Sober:

I FEEL : _____

■ ■

MY GOALS FOR TODAY ARE:

_____

_____

_____

_____

TODAY I'M GRATEFUL FOR:

1.

2.

3.

4.

**I Will Support My
Sobriety Today By:**

DO I FEEL ANY
URGES/CRAVINGS
TODAY?

YES   NO

☐   ☐

today i...

_____

_____

_____

_____

_____

_____

_____

_____

_____

_____

_____

_____

_____

_____

_____

_____

_____

_____

_____

_____

_____

date: _____

DAILY MANTRA:

I'M GROWING
THROUGH WHAT I'M
GOING THROUGH.

Days Sober:

I FEEL : _____

MY GOALS FOR TODAY ARE:

_____
_____
_____
_____
_____

TODAY I'M GRATEFUL FOR:

1.

2.

3.

4.

**I Will Support My
Sobriety Today By:**

DO I FEEL ANY
URGES/CRAVINGS
TODAY?

YES   NO

☐   ☐

today i...

_____
_____
_____
_____
_____
_____
_____
_____
_____
_____
_____
_____
_____
_____
_____
_____
_____
_____
_____

date: _____

DAILY MANTRA:

I AM IN CONTROL
OF MY OWN LIFE.

Days Sober:

I FEEL : _____

■ ■

MY GOALS FOR TODAY ARE:

_____

_____

_____

_____

TODAY I'M GRATEFUL FOR:

1.

2.

3.

4.

**I Will Support My
Sobriety Today By:**

DO I FEEL ANY
URGES/CRAVINGS
TODAY?

YES   NO

today i...

_____
_____
_____
_____
_____
_____
_____
_____
_____
_____
_____
_____
_____
_____
_____
_____
_____
_____
_____

date: _____

EVERY DAY IN
EVERY WAY, I AM
GETTING BETTER.

Days Sober:

I FEEL : _____

■ ■ ■ ■ ■ ■ ■ ■ ■ ■ ■ ■ ■ ■ ■ ■ ■ ■ ■

MY GOALS FOR TODAY ARE:

_____

_____

_____

_____

TODAY I'M GRATEFUL FOR:

1.

2.

3.

4.

I Will Support My Sobriety Today By:

DO I FEEL ANY
URGES/CRAVINGS
TODAY?

YES   NO

☐   ☐

today i...

_____
_____
_____
_____
_____
_____
_____
_____
_____
_____
_____
_____
_____
_____
_____
_____
_____
_____
_____
_____
_____

It's like riding a bike, you know? You have to get your bearing and you have to stay stable. And balanced.

-Edie Falco

date: _____

DAILY MANTRA:

NOTHING CHANGES IF NOTHING CHANGES.

Days Sober:

I FEEL : _____

■ ■ ■ ■ ■ ■ ■ ■ ■ ■ ■ ■ ■ ■ ■ ■

MY GOALS FOR TODAY ARE:

_____

_____

_____

_____

_____

TODAY I'M GRATEFUL FOR:

1.

2.

3.

4.

I Will Support My Sobriety Today By:

DO I FEEL ANY URGES/CRAVINGS TODAY?

YES   NO

today i...

date: _____

DAILY MANTRA:

ONE DAY AT A TIME.

Days Sober:

I FEEL : _____

■ ■

MY GOALS FOR TODAY ARE:

_____
_____
_____
_____
_____

TODAY I'M GRATEFUL FOR:

1.

2.

3.

4.

I Will Support My Sobriety Today By:

DO I FEEL ANY URGES/CRAVINGS TODAY?

YES   NO

today i...

date: _____

DAILY MANTRA:

I'M STRIVING FOR
PROGRESS, NOT
PERFECTION.

Days Sober:

I FEEL : _____

MY GOALS FOR TODAY ARE:

_____
_____
_____
_____
_____

TODAY I'M GRATEFUL FOR:

1.

2.

3.

4.

**I Will Support My
Sobriety Today By:**

DO I FEEL ANY
URGES/CRAVINGS
TODAY?

YES   NO

☐   ☐

today i...

date: _____

DAILY MANTRA:

IF I WANT WHAT I'VE NEVER HAD, I MUST DO WHAT I'VE NEVER DONE.

Days Sober:

I FEEL : _____

■ ■ ■ ■ ■ ■ ■ ■ ■ ■ ■ ■ ■ ■ ■ ■ ■ ■

MY GOALS FOR TODAY ARE:

_____

_____

_____

_____

TODAY I'M GRATEFUL FOR:

1.

2.

3.

4.

I Will Support My Sobriety Today By:

DO I FEEL ANY URGES/CRAVINGS TODAY?

YES   NO

today i...

date: _____

I'M GROWING THROUGH WHAT I'M GOING THROUGH.

Days Sober:

I FEEL : _____

■ ■

MY GOALS FOR TODAY ARE:

_____
_____
_____
_____
_____

TODAY I'M GRATEFUL FOR:

1.

2.

3.

4.

I Will Support My Sobriety Today By:

DO I FEEL ANY URGES/CRAVINGS TODAY?

YES ☐   NO ☐

today i...

_____
_____
_____
_____
_____
_____
_____
_____
_____
_____
_____
_____
_____
_____
_____
_____
_____
_____
_____

date: _____

DAILY MANTRA:

I AM IN CONTROL
OF MY OWN LIFE.

Days Sober:

I FEEL : _____

■ ■ ■ ■ ■ ■ ■ ■ ■ ■ ■ ■ ■ ■ ■ ■ ■ ■ ■ ■

MY GOALS FOR TODAY ARE:

_____

_____

_____

_____

_____

TODAY I'M GRATEFUL FOR:

1.

2.

3.

4.

**I Will Support My
Sobriety Today By:**

DO I FEEL ANY
URGES/CRAVINGS
TODAY?

YES   NO

today i...

_____

_____

_____

_____

_____

_____

_____

_____

_____

_____

_____

_____

_____

_____

_____

_____

_____

_____

_____

date: _____

DAILY MANTRA:

EVERY DAY IN
EVERY WAY, I AM
GETTING BETTER.

Days Sober:

I FEEL : _____

■ ■

MY GOALS FOR TODAY ARE:

_____
_____
_____
_____
_____

TODAY I'M GRATEFUL FOR:

1.

2.

3.

4.

**I Will Support My
Sobriety Today By:**

DO I FEEL ANY
URGES/CRAVINGS
TODAY?

YES   NO

☐   ☐

today i...

What I've learned is that this illness is not something that disappears or fades with time.

-Demi Lovato

date: _____

DAILY MANTRA:

NOTHING CHANGES IF NOTHING CHANGES.

Days Sober:

I FEEL : _____

■ ■ ■ ■ ■ ■ ■ ■ ■ ■ ■ ■ ■ ■ ■ ■ ■ ■ ■ ■

MY GOALS FOR TODAY ARE:

_____
_____
_____
_____
_____

TODAY I'M GRATEFUL FOR:

1.

2.

3.

4.

I Will Support My Sobriety Today By:

DO I FEEL ANY URGES/CRAVINGS TODAY?

YES   NO
☐   ☐

today i...

_____

_____

_____

_____

_____

_____

_____

_____

_____

_____

_____

_____

_____

_____

_____

_____

_____

_____

_____

_____

_____

date: _____

DAILY MANTRA:

ONE DAY AT A TIME.

Days Sober:

I FEEL : _____

■ ■ ■ ■ ■ ■ ■ ■ ■ ■ ■ ■ ■ ■ ■ ■ ■ ■

MY GOALS FOR TODAY ARE:

_____

_____

_____

_____

_____

TODAY I'M GRATEFUL FOR:

1.

2.

3.

4.

I Will Support My Sobriety Today By:

DO I FEEL ANY URGES/CRAVINGS TODAY?

YES   NO

today i...

_____

_____

_____

_____

_____

_____

_____

_____

_____

_____

_____

_____

_____

_____

_____

_____

_____

_____

_____

date: _____

DAILY MANTRA:

I'M STRIVING FOR PROGRESS, NOT PERFECTION.

Days Sober:

I FEEL : _____

■ ■ ■ ■ ■ ■ ■ ■ ■ ■ ■ ■ ■ ■ ■ ■ ■ ■ ■

MY GOALS FOR TODAY ARE:

_____

_____

_____

_____

_____

TODAY I'M GRATEFUL FOR:

1.

2.

3.

4.

I Will Support My Sobriety Today By:

DO I FEEL ANY URGES/CRAVINGS TODAY?

YES   NO

☐   ☐

today i...

date: _____

DAILY MANTRA:

IF I WANT WHAT I'VE
NEVER HAD, I MUST DO
WHAT I'VE NEVER
DONE.

Days Sober:

I FEEL : _____

■ ■ ■ ■ ■ ■ ■ ■ ■ ■ ■ ■ ■ ■ ■ ■ ■ ■ ■ ■

MY GOALS FOR TODAY ARE:

_____
_____
_____
_____

TODAY I'M GRATEFUL FOR:

1.

2.

3.

4.

**I Will Support My
Sobriety Today By:**

DO I FEEL ANY
URGES/CRAVINGS
TODAY?

YES   NO
☐   ☐

today i...

date: _____

I'M GROWING THROUGH WHAT I'M GOING THROUGH.

Days Sober:

I FEEL : _____

■ ■ ■ ■ ■ ■ ■ ■ ■ ■ ■ ■ ■ ■ ■ ■ ■ ■ ■ ■

MY GOALS FOR TODAY ARE:

_____

_____

_____

_____

TODAY I'M GRATEFUL FOR:

1.

2.

3.

4.

I Will Support My Sobriety Today By:

DO I FEEL ANY URGES/CRAVINGS TODAY?

YES   NO

today i...

_____

_____

_____

_____

_____

_____

_____

_____

_____

_____

_____

_____

_____

_____

_____

_____

_____

_____

_____

_____

date: _____

DAILY MANTRA:

I AM IN CONTROL
OF MY OWN LIFE.

Days Sober:

I FEEL : _____

■ ■ ■ ■ ■ ■ ■ ■ ■ ■ ■ ■ ■ ■ ■ ■ ■ ■

MY GOALS FOR TODAY ARE:

_____
_____
_____
_____
_____

TODAY I'M GRATEFUL FOR:

1.

2.

3.

4.

**I Will Support My
Sobriety Today By:**

DO I FEEL ANY
URGES/CRAVINGS
TODAY?

YES   NO

☐   ☐

today i...

_____

_____

_____

_____

_____

_____

_____

_____

_____

_____

_____

_____

_____

_____

_____

_____

_____

_____

_____

_____

date: _____

DAILY MANTRA:

EVERY DAY IN
EVERY WAY, I AM
GETTING BETTER.

Days Sober:

I FEEL : _____

■ ■ ■ ■ ■ ■ ■ ■ ■ ■ ■ ■ ■ ■ ■ ■ ■ ■ ■ ■

MY GOALS FOR TODAY ARE:

_____
_____
_____
_____
_____

TODAY I'M GRATEFUL FOR:

1.

2.

3.

4.

**I Will Support My
Sobriety Today By:**

DO I FEEL ANY
URGES/CRAVINGS
TODAY?

YES   NO

today i...

_____

_____

_____

_____

_____

_____

_____

_____

_____

_____

_____

_____

_____

_____

_____

_____

_____

_____

_____

_____

_____

If you need booze
and drugs to enjoy
your life to the
fullest, then you're
doing it wrong.

-Robin Williams

date: _____

Days Sober:

I FEEL : _____

■ ■

MY GOALS FOR TODAY ARE:

_____
_____
_____
_____
_____

TODAY I'M GRATEFUL FOR:

1.

2.

3.

4.

I Will Support My Sobriety Today By:

DO I FEEL ANY URGES/CRAVINGS TODAY?

YES   NO

☐   ☐

today i...

date:  _____

DAILY MANTRA:

ONE DAY AT A TIME.

Days Sober:

I FEEL : _____

■ ■ ■ ■ ■ ■ ■ ■ ■ ■ ■ ■ ■ ■ ■ ■ ■ ■ ■ ■

MY GOALS FOR TODAY ARE:

_____
_____
_____
_____
_____

TODAY I'M GRATEFUL FOR:

1.

2.

3.

4.

I Will Support My Sobriety Today By:

DO I FEEL ANY URGES/CRAVINGS TODAY?

YES   NO

today i...

_____

_____

_____

_____

_____

_____

_____

_____

_____

_____

_____

_____

_____

_____

_____

_____

_____

_____

_____

_____

date: _____

DAILY MANTRA:

I'M STRIVING FOR PROGRESS, NOT PERFECTION.

Days Sober:

I FEEL : _____

■ ■ ■ ■ ■ ■ ■ ■ ■ ■ ■ ■ ■ ■ ■ ■ ■ ■ ■

MY GOALS FOR TODAY ARE:

_____
_____
_____
_____

TODAY I'M GRATEFUL FOR:

1.

2.

3.

4.

I Will Support My Sobriety Today By:

DO I FEEL ANY URGES/CRAVINGS TODAY?

YES   NO

☐   ☐

today i...

_____
_____
_____
_____
_____
_____
_____
_____
_____
_____
_____
_____
_____
_____
_____
_____
_____
_____
_____
_____

date: _____

DAILY MANTRA:

IF I WANT WHAT I'VE
NEVER HAD, I MUST DO
WHAT I'VE NEVER
DONE.

Days Sober:

I FEEL : _____

■ ■ ■ ■ ■ ■ ■ ■ ■ ■ ■ ■ ■ ■ ■ ■ ■ ■ ■ ■

MY GOALS FOR TODAY ARE:

_____

_____

_____

_____

TODAY I'M GRATEFUL FOR:

1.

2.

3.

4.

**I Will Support My
Sobriety Today By:**

DO I FEEL ANY
URGES/CRAVINGS
TODAY?

YES   NO

☐   ☐

today i...

date: _____

DAILY MANTRA:

I'M GROWING THROUGH WHAT I'M GOING THROUGH.

Days Sober:

I FEEL : _____

■ ■

MY GOALS FOR TODAY ARE:

_____
_____
_____
_____

TODAY I'M GRATEFUL FOR:

1.

2.

3.

4.

I Will Support My Sobriety Today By:

DO I FEEL ANY URGES/CRAVINGS TODAY?

YES   NO

☐   ☐

today i...

_____
_____
_____
_____
_____
_____
_____
_____
_____
_____
_____
_____
_____
_____
_____
_____
_____
_____
_____
_____

date: _____

DAILY MANTRA:

I AM IN CONTROL
OF MY OWN LIFE.

Days Sober:

I FEEL : _____

MY GOALS FOR TODAY ARE:

_____

_____

_____

_____

_____

TODAY I'M GRATEFUL FOR:

1.

2.

3.

4.

**I Will Support My
Sobriety Today By:**

DO I FEEL ANY
URGES/CRAVINGS
TODAY?

YES   NO

today i...

_____

_____

_____

_____

_____

_____

_____

_____

_____

_____

_____

_____

_____

_____

_____

_____

_____

_____

date: _____

DAILY MANTRA:

EVERY DAY IN
EVERY WAY, I AM
GETTING BETTER.

Days Sober:

I FEEL : _____

■ ■

MY GOALS FOR TODAY ARE:

_____
_____
_____
_____

TODAY I'M GRATEFUL FOR:

1.

2.

3.

4.

I Will Support My Sobriety Today By:

DO I FEEL ANY URGES/CRAVINGS TODAY?

YES   NO

today i...

_____
_____
_____
_____
_____
_____
_____
_____
_____
_____
_____
_____
_____
_____
_____
_____
_____
_____
_____
_____

At one point, I could never have conceived going out and not drinking but, as time goes on, you lose the urge and the insecurity that often makes people drink in the first place.

-Gerard Butler

date: _____

NOTHING CHANGES
IF NOTHING
CHANGES.

Days Sober:

I FEEL : _____

MY GOALS FOR TODAY ARE:

_____

_____

_____

_____

TODAY I'M GRATEFUL FOR:

1.

2.

3.

4.

**I Will Support My
Sobriety Today By:**

DO I FEEL ANY
URGES/CRAVINGS
TODAY?

YES   NO

today i...

_____
_____
_____
_____
_____
_____
_____
_____
_____
_____
_____
_____
_____
_____
_____
_____
_____
_____

date: _____

DAILY MANTRA:

ONE DAY AT A TIME.

Days Sober:

I FEEL : _____

■ ■

MY GOALS FOR TODAY ARE:

_____

_____

_____

_____

_____

TODAY I'M GRATEFUL FOR:

1.

2.

3.

4.

I Will Support My Sobriety Today By:

DO I FEEL ANY URGES/CRAVINGS TODAY?

YES   NO

☐   ☐

today i...

_____

_____

_____

_____

_____

_____

_____

_____

_____

_____

_____

_____

_____

_____

_____

_____

_____

_____

date: _____

DAILY MANTRA:

I'M STRIVING FOR PROGRESS, NOT PERFECTION.

Days Sober:

I FEEL : _____

∎ ∎

MY GOALS FOR TODAY ARE:

_____

_____

_____

_____

_____

TODAY I'M GRATEFUL FOR:

1.

2.

3.

4.

I Will Support My Sobriety Today By:

DO I FEEL ANY URGES/CRAVINGS TODAY?

YES   NO

☐   ☐

today i...

_____
_____
_____
_____
_____
_____
_____
_____
_____
_____
_____
_____
_____
_____
_____
_____
_____
_____

date: _____

DAILY MANTRA:

IF I WANT WHAT I'VE
NEVER HAD, I MUST DO
WHAT I'VE NEVER
DONE.

Days Sober:

I FEEL : _____

■ ■ ■ ■ ■ ■ ■ ■ ■ ■ ■ ■ ■ ■ ■ ■ ■ ■ ■ ■

MY GOALS FOR TODAY ARE:

_____

_____

_____

_____

_____

TODAY I'M GRATEFUL FOR:

1.

2.

3.

4.

**I Will Support My
Sobriety Today By:**

DO I FEEL ANY
URGES/CRAVINGS
TODAY?

YES   NO

today i...

_____

_____

_____

_____

_____

_____

_____

_____

_____

_____

_____

_____

_____

_____

_____

_____

_____

_____

_____

_____

date: _____

I'M GROWING THROUGH WHAT I'M GOING THROUGH.

Days Sober:

I FEEL : _____

■ ■ ■ ■ ■ ■ ■ ■ ■ ■ ■ ■ ■ ■ ■ ■ ■

MY GOALS FOR TODAY ARE:

_____
_____
_____
_____
_____

TODAY I'M GRATEFUL FOR:

1.

2.

3.

4.

I Will Support My Sobriety Today By:

DO I FEEL ANY URGES/CRAVINGS TODAY?

YES   NO

☐   ☐

today i...

_____
_____
_____
_____
_____
_____
_____
_____
_____
_____
_____
_____
_____
_____
_____
_____
_____
_____
_____
_____
_____
_____

date: _____

DAILY MANTRA:

I AM IN CONTROL
OF MY OWN LIFE.

Days Sober:

I FEEL : _____

■ ■ ■ ■ ■ ■ ■ ■ ■ ■ ■ ■ ■ ■ ■ ■ ■ ■ ■ ■

MY GOALS FOR TODAY ARE:

_____

_____

_____

_____

_____

TODAY I'M GRATEFUL FOR:

1.

2.

3.

4.

**I Will Support My
Sobriety Today By:**

DO I FEEL ANY
URGES/CRAVINGS
TODAY?

YES   NO

today i...

date: _____

DAILY MANTRA:

EVERY DAY IN
EVERY WAY, I AM
GETTING BETTER.

Days Sober:

I FEEL : _____

MY GOALS FOR TODAY ARE:

_____
_____
_____
_____
_____

TODAY I'M GRATEFUL FOR:

1.

2.

3.

4.

**I Will Support My
Sobriety Today By:**

DO I FEEL ANY
URGES/CRAVINGS
TODAY?

YES   NO

☐   ☐

today i...

_____
_____
_____
_____
_____
_____
_____
_____
_____
_____
_____
_____
_____
_____
_____
_____
_____
_____
_____
_____

I have never
regretted not
drinking. Say this
to yourself, and
you'll get through
anything.

-Meredith Bell

date: _____

DAILY MANTRA:

NOTHING CHANGES
IF NOTHING
CHANGES.

Days Sober:

I FEEL : _____

■ ■

MY GOALS FOR TODAY ARE:

_____

_____

_____

_____

_____

TODAY I'M GRATEFUL FOR:

1.

2.

3.

4.

**I Will Support My
Sobriety Today By:**

DO I FEEL ANY
URGES/CRAVINGS
TODAY?

YES   NO

☐   ☐

today i...

_____
_____
_____
_____
_____
_____
_____
_____
_____
_____
_____
_____
_____
_____
_____
_____
_____
_____
_____
_____

date: _____

DAILY MANTRA:

ONE DAY AT A TIME.

Days Sober:

I FEEL : _____

■ ■ ■ ■ ■ ■ ■ ■ ■ ■ ■ ■ ■ ■ ■ ■ ■ ■ ■ ■

MY GOALS FOR TODAY ARE:

_____

_____

_____

_____

_____

TODAY I'M GRATEFUL FOR:

1.

2.

3.

4.

I Will Support My Sobriety Today By:

DO I FEEL ANY URGES/CRAVINGS TODAY?

YES   NO

today i...

date: _____

I'M STRIVING FOR PROGRESS, NOT PERFECTION.

Days Sober:

I FEEL : _____

■ ■

MY GOALS FOR TODAY ARE:

_____
_____
_____
_____
_____

TODAY I'M GRATEFUL FOR:

1.

2.

3.

4.

I Will Support My Sobriety Today By:

DO I FEEL ANY URGES/CRAVINGS TODAY?

YES   NO

today i...

_____
_____
_____
_____
_____
_____
_____
_____
_____
_____
_____
_____
_____
_____
_____
_____
_____
_____
_____
_____
_____

date: _____

DAILY MANTRA:

IF I WANT WHAT I'VE NEVER HAD, I MUST DO WHAT I'VE NEVER DONE.

Days Sober:

I FEEL : _____

■ ■ ■ ■ ■ ■ ■ ■ ■ ■ ■ ■ ■ ■ ■ ■ ■ ■

MY GOALS FOR TODAY ARE:

_____
_____
_____
_____
_____

TODAY I'M GRATEFUL FOR:

1.

2.

3.

4.

I Will Support My Sobriety Today By:

DO I FEEL ANY URGES/CRAVINGS TODAY?

YES   NO

today i...

_____

_____

_____

_____

_____

_____

_____

_____

_____

_____

_____

_____

_____

_____

_____

_____

_____

_____

_____

date: _____

DAILY MANTRA:

I'M GROWING THROUGH WHAT I'M GOING THROUGH.

Days Sober:

I FEEL : _____

■ ■ ■ ■ ■ ■ ■ ■ ■ ■ ■ ■ ■ ■ ■ ■ ■ ■ ■ ■

MY GOALS FOR TODAY ARE:

_____
_____
_____
_____
_____

TODAY I'M GRATEFUL FOR:

1.

2.

3.

4.

I Will Support My Sobriety Today By:

DO I FEEL ANY URGES/CRAVINGS TODAY?

YES   NO

☐   ☐

today i...

_____
_____
_____
_____
_____
_____
_____
_____
_____
_____
_____
_____
_____
_____
_____
_____
_____
_____
_____
_____

date:  _____

DAILY MANTRA:

I AM IN CONTROL
OF MY OWN LIFE.

Days Sober:

I FEEL : _____

■ ■ ■ ■ ■ ■ ■ ■ ■ ■ ■ ■ ■ ■ ■ ■ ■ ■ ■

MY GOALS FOR TODAY ARE:

_____

_____

_____

_____

_____

TODAY I'M GRATEFUL FOR:

1.

2.

3.

4.

**I Will Support My
Sobriety Today By:**

DO I FEEL ANY
URGES/CRAVINGS
TODAY?

YES   NO

today i...

_____
_____
_____
_____
_____
_____
_____
_____
_____
_____
_____
_____
_____
_____
_____
_____
_____
_____

date: _____

DAILY MANTRA:

EVERY DAY IN EVERY WAY, I AM GETTING BETTER.

Days Sober:

I FEEL : _____

■ ■ ■ ■ ■ ■ ■ ■ ■ ■ ■ ■ ■ ■ ■ ■ ■ ■ ■ ■

MY GOALS FOR TODAY ARE:

_____
_____
_____
_____
_____

TODAY I'M GRATEFUL FOR:

1.

2.

3.

4.

I Will Support My Sobriety Today By:

DO I FEEL ANY URGES/CRAVINGS TODAY?

YES   NO

☐   ☐

today i...

_____

_____

_____

_____

_____

_____

_____

_____

_____

_____

_____

_____

_____

_____

_____

_____

_____

_____

_____

_____

_____

My main focus in sobriety has been to replace fear with faith or love.

-Steve-O

date: _____

DAILY MANTRA:

NOTHING CHANGES
IF NOTHING
CHANGES.

Days Sober:

I FEEL : _____

■ ■ ■ ■ ■ ■ ■ ■ ■ ■ ■ ■ ■ ■ ■ ■ ■ ■ ■ ■

MY GOALS FOR TODAY ARE:

_____
_____
_____
_____
_____

TODAY I'M GRATEFUL FOR:

1.

2.

3.

4.

**I Will Support My
Sobriety Today By:**

DO I FEEL ANY
URGES/CRAVINGS
TODAY?

YES   NO

☐   ☐

today i...

date: _____

DAILY MANTRA:

ONE DAY AT A TIME.

Days Sober:

I FEEL : _____

■ ■ ■ ■ ■ ■ ■ ■ ■ ■ ■ ■ ■ ■ ■ ■ ■ ■ ■ ■

MY GOALS FOR TODAY ARE:

_____

_____

_____

_____

_____

TODAY I'M GRATEFUL FOR:

1.

2.

3.

4.

I Will Support My Sobriety Today By:

DO I FEEL ANY URGES/CRAVINGS TODAY?

YES   NO

☐   ☐

today i...

_____

_____

_____

_____

_____

_____

_____

_____

_____

_____

_____

_____

_____

_____

_____

_____

_____

_____

_____

date: _____

DAILY MANTRA:

I'M STRIVING FOR
PROGRESS, NOT
PERFECTION.

Days Sober:

I FEEL : _____

■ ■ ■ ■ ■ ■ ■ ■ ■ ■ ■ ■ ■ ■ ■ ■ ■ ■ ■

MY GOALS FOR TODAY ARE:

_____

_____

_____

_____

TODAY I'M GRATEFUL FOR:

1.

2.

3.

4.

**I Will Support My
Sobriety Today By:**

DO I FEEL ANY
URGES/CRAVINGS
TODAY?

YES   NO

☐   ☐

today i...

_____

_____

_____

_____

_____

_____

_____

_____

_____

_____

_____

_____

_____

_____

_____

_____

_____

date:  _____

DAILY MANTRA:

IF I WANT WHAT I'VE
NEVER HAD, I MUST DO
WHAT I'VE NEVER
DONE.

Days Sober:

I FEEL : _____

■ ■ ■ ■ ■ ■ ■ ■ ■ ■ ■ ■ ■ ■ ■ ■ ■ ■ ■ ■

MY GOALS FOR TODAY ARE:

_____
_____
_____
_____
_____

TODAY I'M GRATEFUL FOR:

1.

2.

3.

4.

**I Will Support My
Sobriety Today By:**

DO I FEEL ANY
URGES/CRAVINGS
TODAY?

YES   NO

☐   ☐

today i...

_____
_____
_____
_____
_____
_____
_____
_____
_____
_____
_____
_____
_____
_____
_____
_____
_____
_____

date: _____

DAILY MANTRA:

I'M GROWING
THROUGH WHAT I'M
GOING THROUGH.

Days Sober:

I FEEL : _____

■ ■ ■ ■ ■ ■ ■ ■ ■ ■ ■ ■ ■ ■ ■ ■ ■ ■ ■

MY GOALS FOR TODAY ARE:

_____
_____
_____
_____

TODAY I'M GRATEFUL FOR:

1.

2.

3.

4.

**I Will Support My
Sobriety Today By:**

DO I FEEL ANY
URGES/CRAVINGS
TODAY?

YES   NO

☐   ☐

today i...

**date:** _____

DAILY MANTRA:

I AM IN CONTROL
OF MY OWN LIFE.

Days Sober:

I FEEL : _____

■ ■

MY GOALS FOR TODAY ARE:

_____
_____
_____
_____
_____

TODAY I'M GRATEFUL FOR:

1.

2.

3.

4.

**I Will Support My
Sobriety Today By:**

DO I FEEL ANY
URGES/CRAVINGS
TODAY?

YES   NO

today i...

_____

_____

_____

_____

_____

_____

_____

_____

_____

_____

_____

_____

_____

_____

_____

_____

_____

date: _____

DAILY MANTRA:

EVERY DAY IN
EVERY WAY, I AM
GETTING BETTER.

Days Sober:

I FEEL : _____

■ ■

MY GOALS FOR TODAY ARE:

_____
_____
_____
_____
_____

TODAY I'M GRATEFUL FOR:

1.

2.

3.

4.

**I Will Support My
Sobriety Today By:**

DO I FEEL ANY
URGES/CRAVINGS
TODAY?

YES   NO

☐   ☐

today i...

_____

_____

_____

_____

_____

_____

_____

_____

_____

_____

_____

_____

_____

_____

_____

_____

_____

_____

_____

_____

_____

No matter how dark
the night may get,
your light will never
burn out.

-Jeanette LeBlanc

date: _____

DAILY MANTRA:

NOTHING CHANGES IF NOTHING CHANGES.

Days Sober:

I FEEL : _____

■ ■ ■ ■ ■ ■ ■ ■ ■ ■ ■ ■ ■ ■ ■ ■ ■ ■ ■ ■

MY GOALS FOR TODAY ARE:

_____
_____
_____
_____
_____

TODAY I'M GRATEFUL FOR:

1.

2.

3.

4.

I Will Support My Sobriety Today By:

DO I FEEL ANY URGES/CRAVINGS TODAY?

YES   NO

today i...

_____

_____

_____

_____

_____

_____

_____

_____

_____

_____

_____

_____

_____

_____

_____

_____

_____

_____

_____

_____

_____

date: _____

DAILY MANTRA:

ONE DAY AT A TIME.

Days Sober:

I FEEL : _____

MY GOALS FOR TODAY ARE:

_____

_____

_____

_____

_____

TODAY I'M GRATEFUL FOR:

1.

2.

3.

4.

I Will Support My Sobriety Today By:

DO I FEEL ANY URGES/CRAVINGS TODAY?

YES ☐   NO ☐

today i...

_____

_____

_____

_____

_____

_____

_____

_____

_____

_____

_____

_____

_____

_____

_____

_____

_____

_____

_____

_____

date:  _____

DAILY MANTRA:

I'M STRIVING FOR
PROGRESS, NOT
PERFECTION.

Days Sober:

I FEEL : _____

■ ■ ■ ■ ■ ■ ■ ■ ■ ■ ■ ■ ■ ■ ■ ■ ■ ■ ■

MY GOALS FOR TODAY ARE:

_____
_____
_____
_____
_____

TODAY I'M GRATEFUL FOR:

1.

2.

3.

4.

**I Will Support My
Sobriety Today By:**

DO I FEEL ANY
URGES/CRAVINGS
TODAY?

YES   NO

☐   ☐

today i...

_____

_____

_____

_____

_____

_____

_____

_____

_____

_____

_____

_____

_____

_____

_____

_____

_____

_____

_____

_____

_____

_____

date: _____

DAILY MANTRA:

IF I WANT WHAT I'VE
NEVER HAD, I MUST DO
WHAT I'VE NEVER
DONE.

Days Sober:

I FEEL : _____

MY GOALS FOR TODAY ARE:

_____

_____

_____

_____

_____

TODAY I'M GRATEFUL FOR:

1.

2.

3.

4.

**I Will Support My
Sobriety Today By:**

DO I FEEL ANY
URGES/CRAVINGS
TODAY?

YES   NO

today i...

_____

_____

_____

_____

_____

_____

_____

_____

_____

_____

_____

_____

_____

_____

_____

_____

_____

_____

_____

_____

date: _____

DAILY MANTRA:

I'M GROWING THROUGH WHAT I'M GOING THROUGH.

Days Sober:

I FEEL : _____

MY GOALS FOR TODAY ARE:

_____

_____

_____

_____

TODAY I'M GRATEFUL FOR:

1.

2.

3.

4.

I Will Support My Sobriety Today By:

DO I FEEL ANY URGES/CRAVINGS TODAY?

YES

NO

today i...

date: _____

DAILY MANTRA:

I AM IN CONTROL
OF MY OWN LIFE.

Days Sober:

I FEEL : _____

■ ■ ■ ■ ■ ■ ■ ■ ■ ■ ■ ■ ■ ■ ■ ■ ■ ■ ■

MY GOALS FOR TODAY ARE:

_____
_____
_____
_____
_____

TODAY I'M GRATEFUL FOR:

1.

2.

3.

4.

**I Will Support My
Sobriety Today By:**

DO I FEEL ANY
URGES/CRAVINGS
TODAY?

YES   NO

☐   ☐

today i...

_____
_____
_____
_____
_____
_____
_____
_____
_____
_____
_____
_____
_____
_____
_____
_____
_____
_____
_____
_____
_____
_____

date: _____

DAILY MANTRA:

EVERY DAY IN EVERY WAY, I AM GETTING BETTER.

Days Sober:

I FEEL : _____

■ ■ ■ ■ ■ ■ ■ ■ ■ ■ ■ ■ ■ ■ ■ ■ ■ ■ ■

MY GOALS FOR TODAY ARE:

_____

_____

_____

_____

TODAY I'M GRATEFUL FOR:

1.

2.

3.

4.

I Will Support My Sobriety Today By:

DO I FEEL ANY URGES/CRAVINGS TODAY?

YES   NO

☐   ☐

today i...

_____

_____

_____

_____

_____

_____

_____

_____

_____

_____

_____

_____

_____

_____

_____

_____

_____

_____

_____

_____

Recovery is an acceptance that your life is in shambles and you have to change.

-Jamie Lee Curtis

date: _____

NOTHING CHANGES IF NOTHING CHANGES.

Days Sober:

I FEEL : _____

■ ■

MY GOALS FOR TODAY ARE:

_____

_____

_____

_____

_____

TODAY I'M GRATEFUL FOR:

1.

2.

3.

4.

I Will Support My Sobriety Today By:

DO I FEEL ANY URGES/CRAVINGS TODAY?

YES   NO

☐   ☐

today i...

_____

_____

_____

_____

_____

_____

_____

_____

_____

_____

_____

_____

_____

_____

_____

_____

_____

_____

_____

_____

date: _____

DAILY MANTRA:

ONE DAY AT A TIME.

Days Sober:

I FEEL : _____

■ ■ ■ ■ ■ ■ ■ ■ ■ ■ ■ ■ ■ ■ ■ ■ ■ ■ ■ ■

MY GOALS FOR TODAY ARE:

_____
_____
_____
_____
_____

TODAY I'M GRATEFUL FOR:

1.

2.

3.

4.

I Will Support My Sobriety Today By:

DO I FEEL ANY URGES/CRAVINGS TODAY?

YES   NO

today i...

_____
_____
_____
_____
_____
_____
_____
_____
_____
_____
_____
_____
_____
_____
_____
_____
_____
_____
_____
_____

date: _____

DAILY MANTRA:

I'M STRIVING FOR
PROGRESS, NOT
PERFECTION.

Days Sober:

I FEEL : _____

MY GOALS FOR TODAY ARE:

_____
_____
_____
_____
_____

TODAY I'M GRATEFUL FOR:

1.

2.

3.

4.

**I Will Support My
Sobriety Today By:**

DO I FEEL ANY
URGES/CRAVINGS
TODAY?

YES   NO

today i...

_____
_____
_____
_____
_____
_____
_____
_____
_____
_____
_____
_____
_____
_____
_____
_____
_____
_____
_____

date: _____

DAILY MANTRA:

IF I WANT WHAT I'VE
NEVER HAD, I MUST DO
WHAT I'VE NEVER
DONE.

Days Sober:

I FEEL : _____

■ ■

MY GOALS FOR TODAY ARE:

_____

_____

_____

_____

_____

TODAY I'M GRATEFUL FOR:

1.

2.

3.

4.

**I Will Support My
Sobriety Today By:**

DO I FEEL ANY
URGES/CRAVINGS
TODAY?

YES   NO

☐   ☐

today i...

_____

_____

_____

_____

_____

_____

_____

_____

_____

_____

_____

_____

_____

_____

_____

_____

_____

_____

_____

_____

date: _____

DAILY MANTRA:

I'M GROWING
THROUGH WHAT I'M
GOING THROUGH.

Days Sober:

I FEEL : _____

MY GOALS FOR TODAY ARE:

_____
_____
_____
_____

TODAY I'M GRATEFUL FOR:

1.

2.

3.

4.

**I Will Support My
Sobriety Today By:**

DO I FEEL ANY
URGES/CRAVINGS
TODAY?

YES   NO

☐   ☐

today i...

date: _____

DAILY MANTRA:

I AM IN CONTROL
OF MY OWN LIFE.

Days Sober:

I FEEL : _____

MY GOALS FOR TODAY ARE:

_____

_____

_____

_____

TODAY I'M GRATEFUL FOR:

1.

2.

3.

4.

**I Will Support My
Sobriety Today By:**

DO I FEEL ANY
URGES/CRAVINGS
TODAY?

YES   NO

today i...

_____
_____
_____
_____
_____
_____
_____
_____
_____
_____
_____
_____
_____
_____
_____
_____
_____
_____
_____

date: _____

DAILY MANTRA:

EVERY DAY IN
EVERY WAY, I AM
GETTING BETTER.

Days Sober:

I FEEL : _____

MY GOALS FOR TODAY ARE:

_____
_____
_____
_____
_____

TODAY I'M GRATEFUL FOR:

1.

2.

3.

4.

I Will Support My
Sobriety Today By:

DO I FEEL ANY
URGES/CRAVINGS
TODAY?

YES   NO

☐   ☐

today i...

_____

_____

_____

_____

_____

_____

_____

_____

_____

_____

_____

_____

_____

_____

_____

_____

_____

_____

_____

_____

Being in recovery has given me everything of value that I have in my life. Integrity, honesty, fearlessness, faith, a relationship with God, and most of all, gratitude.

-Rob Lowe

date: _____

NOTHING CHANGES
IF NOTHING
CHANGES.

Days Sober:

I FEEL : _____

■ ■ ■ ■ ■ ■ ■ ■ ■ ■ ■ ■ ■ ■ ■ ■ ■ ■ ■ ■

MY GOALS FOR TODAY ARE:

_____
_____
_____
_____
_____

TODAY I'M GRATEFUL FOR:

1.

2.

3.

4.

**I Will Support My
Sobriety Today By:**

DO I FEEL ANY
URGES/CRAVINGS
TODAY?

YES   NO

☐   ☐

today i...

_____

_____

_____

_____

_____

_____

_____

_____

_____

_____

_____

_____

_____

_____

_____

_____

_____

_____

_____

_____

_____

_____

date: _____

DAILY MANTRA:

ONE DAY AT A TIME.

Days Sober:

I FEEL : _____

■ ■ ■ ■ ■ ■ ■ ■ ■ ■ ■ ■ ■ ■ ■ ■ ■ ■ ■ ■

MY GOALS FOR TODAY ARE:

_____
_____
_____
_____
_____

TODAY I'M GRATEFUL FOR:

1.

2.

3.

4.

I Will Support My Sobriety Today By:

DO I FEEL ANY URGES/CRAVINGS TODAY?

YES   NO

☐   ☐

today i...

_____
_____
_____
_____
_____
_____
_____
_____
_____
_____
_____
_____
_____
_____
_____
_____
_____
_____
_____
_____
_____

date: _____

DAILY MANTRA:

I'M STRIVING FOR PROGRESS, NOT PERFECTION.

Days Sober:

I FEEL : _____

■ ■

MY GOALS FOR TODAY ARE:

_____

_____

_____

_____

_____

TODAY I'M GRATEFUL FOR:

1.

2.

3.

4.

I Will Support My Sobriety Today By:

DO I FEEL ANY URGES/CRAVINGS TODAY?

YES   NO

☐   ☐

today i...

_____
_____
_____
_____
_____
_____
_____
_____
_____
_____
_____
_____
_____
_____
_____
_____
_____
_____
_____
_____
_____
_____

date: _____

DAILY MANTRA:

IF I WANT WHAT I'VE
NEVER HAD, I MUST DO
WHAT I'VE NEVER
DONE.

Days Sober:

I FEEL : _____

■ ■ ■ ■ ■ ■ ■ ■ ■ ■ ■ ■ ■ ■ ■ ■ ■ ■ ■ ■

MY GOALS FOR TODAY ARE:

_____

_____

_____

_____

_____

TODAY I'M GRATEFUL FOR:

1.

2.

3.

4.

**I Will Support My
Sobriety Today By:**

DO I FEEL ANY
URGES/CRAVINGS
TODAY?

YES   NO

☐   ☐

today i...

_____
_____
_____
_____
_____
_____
_____
_____
_____
_____
_____
_____
_____
_____
_____
_____
_____
_____
_____
_____
_____
_____

date: _____

DAILY MANTRA:

I'M GROWING THROUGH WHAT I'M GOING THROUGH.

Days Sober:

I FEEL : _____

■ ■ ■ ■ ■ ■ ■ ■ ■ ■ ■ ■ ■ ■ ■ ■ ■ ■ ■ ■

MY GOALS FOR TODAY ARE:

_____
_____
_____
_____
_____

TODAY I'M GRATEFUL FOR:

1.

2.

3.

4.

I Will Support My Sobriety Today By:

DO I FEEL ANY URGES/CRAVINGS TODAY?

YES   NO

☐   ☐

today i...

_____
_____
_____
_____
_____
_____
_____
_____
_____
_____
_____
_____
_____
_____
_____
_____
_____
_____
_____
_____
_____

date: _____

DAILY MANTRA:

I AM IN CONTROL
OF MY OWN LIFE.

Days Sober:

I FEEL : _____

MY GOALS FOR TODAY ARE:

_____

_____

_____

_____

_____

TODAY I'M GRATEFUL FOR:

1.

2.

3.

4.

**I Will Support My
Sobriety Today By:**

DO I FEEL ANY
URGES/CRAVINGS
TODAY?

YES   NO

today i...

_____

_____

_____

_____

_____

_____

_____

_____

_____

_____

_____

_____

_____

_____

_____

_____

_____

_____

date: _____

DAILY MANTRA:

EVERY DAY IN
EVERY WAY, I AM
GETTING BETTER.

Days Sober:

I FEEL : _____

■ ■ ■ ■ ■ ■ ■ ■ ■ ■ ■ ■ ■ ■ ■ ■ ■ ■ ■ ■

MY GOALS FOR TODAY ARE:

_____

_____

_____

_____

_____

TODAY I'M GRATEFUL FOR:

1.

2.

3.

4.

**I Will Support My
Sobriety Today By:**

DO I FEEL ANY
URGES/CRAVINGS
TODAY?

YES   NO

today i...

_____

_____

_____

_____

_____

_____

_____

_____

_____

_____

_____

_____

_____

_____

_____

_____

_____

_____

_____

Though no one can
go back and make a
brand new start,
anyone can start
from now and make
a brand new ending.

-Carl Bard

date: _____

DAILY MANTRA:

NOTHING CHANGES IF NOTHING CHANGES.

Days Sober:

I FEEL : _____

∎ ∎ ∎ ∎ ∎ ∎ ∎ ∎ ∎ ∎ ∎ ∎ ∎ ∎ ∎ ∎

MY GOALS FOR TODAY ARE:

_____

_____

_____

_____

TODAY I'M GRATEFUL FOR:

1.

2.

3.

4.

I Will Support My Sobriety Today By:

DO I FEEL ANY URGES/CRAVINGS TODAY?

YES   NO

☐   ☐

today i...

_____

_____

_____

_____

_____

_____

_____

_____

_____

_____

_____

_____

_____

_____

_____

_____

_____

_____

_____

date: _____

DAILY MANTRA:

ONE DAY AT A TIME.

Days Sober:

I FEEL : _____

■ ■ ■ ■ ■ ■ ■ ■ ■ ■ ■ ■ ■ ■ ■ ■ ■ ■ ■

MY GOALS FOR TODAY ARE:

_____
_____
_____
_____
_____

TODAY I'M GRATEFUL FOR:

1.

2.

3.

4.

I Will Support My Sobriety Today By:

DO I FEEL ANY URGES/CRAVINGS TODAY?

YES   NO

☐   ☐

today i...

_____

_____

_____

_____

_____

_____

_____

_____

_____

_____

_____

_____

_____

_____

_____

_____

_____

_____

_____

_____

_____

_____

date: _____

DAILY MANTRA:

I'M STRIVING FOR PROGRESS, NOT PERFECTION.

Days Sober:

I FEEL : _____

■ ■ ■ ■ ■ ■ ■ ■ ■ ■ ■ ■ ■ ■ ■ ■ ■ ■ ■

MY GOALS FOR TODAY ARE:

_____

_____

_____

_____

TODAY I'M GRATEFUL FOR:

1.

2.

3.

4.

I Will Support My Sobriety Today By:

DO I FEEL ANY URGES/CRAVINGS TODAY?

YES   NO

☐   ☐

today i...

_____

_____

_____

_____

_____

_____

_____

_____

_____

_____

_____

_____

_____

_____

_____

_____

_____

_____

_____

_____

date: _____

Days Sober:

I FEEL : _____

■ ■ ■ ■ ■ ■ ■ ■ ■ ■ ■ ■ ■ ■ ■ ■ ■ ■ ■

MY GOALS FOR TODAY ARE:

_____
_____
_____
_____
_____

TODAY I'M GRATEFUL FOR:

1.

2.

3.

4.

I Will Support My Sobriety Today By:

DO I FEEL ANY URGES/CRAVINGS TODAY?

YES   NO

☐   ☐

today i...

_____

_____

_____

_____

_____

_____

_____

_____

_____

_____

_____

_____

_____

_____

_____

_____

_____

_____

_____

_____

date: _____

DAILY MANTRA:

I'M GROWING THROUGH WHAT I'M GOING THROUGH.

Days Sober:

I FEEL : _____

MY GOALS FOR TODAY ARE:

_____

_____

_____

_____

TODAY I'M GRATEFUL FOR:

1.

2.

3.

4.

I Will Support My Sobriety Today By:

DO I FEEL ANY URGES/CRAVINGS TODAY?

YES   NO

today i...

_____

_____

_____

_____

_____

_____

_____

_____

_____

_____

_____

_____

_____

_____

_____

_____

_____

_____

_____

_____

_____

date: _____

DAILY MANTRA:

I AM IN CONTROL
OF MY OWN LIFE.

Days Sober:

I FEEL : _____

■ ■ ■ ■ ■ ■ ■ ■ ■ ■ ■ ■ ■ ■ ■ ■ ■ ■ ■

MY GOALS FOR TODAY ARE:

_____
_____
_____
_____
_____

TODAY I'M GRATEFUL FOR:

1.

2.

3.

4.

**I Will Support My
Sobriety Today By:**

DO I FEEL ANY
URGES/CRAVINGS
TODAY?

YES   NO

☐   ☐

today i...

_____

_____

_____

_____

_____

_____

_____

_____

_____

_____

_____

_____

_____

_____

_____

_____

_____

_____

_____

_____

_____

date:

DAILY MANTRA:

EVERY DAY IN
EVERY WAY, I AM
GETTING BETTER.

Days Sober:

I FEEL : _____

■ ■ ■ ■ ■ ■ ■ ■ ■ ■ ■ ■ ■ ■ ■ ■ ■ ■ ■

MY GOALS FOR TODAY ARE:

_____
_____
_____
_____

TODAY I'M GRATEFUL FOR:

1.

2.

3.

4.

**I Will Support My
Sobriety Today By:**

DO I FEEL ANY
URGES/CRAVINGS
TODAY?

YES   NO

☐   ☐

today i...

_____
_____
_____
_____
_____
_____
_____
_____
_____
_____
_____
_____
_____
_____
_____
_____
_____
_____
_____
_____

Resources

National Council for Alcohol and Drug Dependence Inc.
NCADD.org
24 Hour Hope Line: 1-800-622-2255

**Substance Abuse and Mental Health Services
Administration**
SAMHSA.gov
24 Hour National Helpline: 1-800-622-HELP(4357)

Alcoholics Anonymous
AA.org
Information on Online Groups/Meetings: AA-intergroup.org

Suicide Prevention Hotline
www.suicidepreventionlifeline.org
24 Hour Hotline: 1-800-273-TALK (8255)

Al-Anon Family Groups
AL-ANON.org
Meeting Line: 888-425-2666

About The Author

As an entrepreneur, makeup artist, self-published author, YouTuber, mindset coach, podcast host, and blogger, Sarah Ordo is your not-so-average Millennial craving to leave her mark on this world in more ways than one.

Sarah's award-winning on location hair and makeup company (based out of Detroit), 24Luxe Hair & Makeup, has been styling women for their special events since 2013. Her social media pages reach thousands of followers daily featuring a variety of beauty, health, lifestyle, sobriety, and wellness posts. Her YouTube videos documenting and following her sobriety have reached millions of viewers internationally, and have even been featured on Dateline NBC. Sarah has been featured on and interviewed for numerous blogs and podcasts including Cara Alwill Leyba's Style Your Mind Podcast and Courtney Bentley's Fit Fierce & Fabulous Podcast.

On her podcast Her Best F***ing Life, Sarah loves to talk about all topics surrounding how to create a life you love, your best life possible. The episodes feature a no-bullsh*t approach to life, amazing guest interviews, and a whole lot of swearing. On her website, sarahordo.com, Sarah blogs about living sober, self-love, mental health, and many other raw, honest topics. She also sells merchandise on her website for her books and podcast.

*Sober as F*** was the first full-length memoir and book written by Sarah, released in May 2017. She has gone on to publish Innerbloom, *Sober As F***:The Workbook*, the *Her Best F***ing Life Planner*, *Thirty as F***, and *32 Bada$$ Things About Being Sober,* which are all available on Amazon & Kindle.

Connect with Sarah: www.sarahordo.com
Youtube: Sarah Ordo
Instagram: @24Luxe_Sarah
Podcast: Her Best F*ing Life (on iTunes & Stitcher)**
Books: Amazon & Kindle

Made in the USA
Las Vegas, NV
29 November 2022